11+ Mock Exam

MEC-15-001-A

Multiple-Choice Question Paper

Read the following carefully:

- There are three sections in this paper.
- You have 50 minutes in total to complete this paper. The time allowed for each section is given at the beginning of that section
- There are 80 questions in this paper and each question is worth 1 mark.
- You may work out the answers on a rough sheet of paper.
- The answers should be marked on the answer sheet provided as shown below. Do not mark your answers on the question paper.
- Make sure you mark the answer in the correct column matching the question number.
- If you make a mistake, rub out the answer completely before marking.
- You should only mark one answer for each question.
- If you find a question difficult, do not spend too much time on it. Move on to the next question and come back to it later.

80 Multiple Choice Questions to be completed in 50 minutes

QE Learning

www.QELearning.co.uk

PART 1

NUMERICAL REASONING - 25 MINUTES (30 QUESTIONS)

Section 1 - Numerical Reasoning (30 Questions)

Answer the questions by selecting one answer from the options A-E. Mark your answer on the answer sheet.

1 Look at the shape below. The height and width of the shape are as shown in the figure in CM. If the width of the shape is HALVED and the height of the shape is DOUBLED, then what is the AREA of the new shape in CM^2?

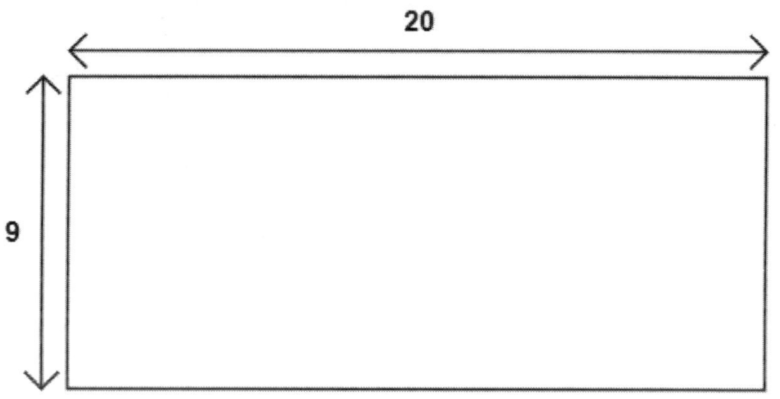

A	B	C	D	E
178 SQ CM	177 SQ CM	180 SQ CM	179 SQ CM	184 SQ CM

2 The perimeter of a face of a square cube is 36 Centimetres. What is its volume?

A	B	C	D	E
729 Cm^3	59049 Cm^3	6561 Cm^3	531441 Cm^3	81 Cm^3

3 A Builder used SQUARE tiles to cover a rectangular surface. Each side of the square tile was 10 cm and he used 1804 tiles to cover the surface. There were 41 tiles along one of the sides of the surface. What was the PERIMETER of the surface covered by the tiles?

A	B	C	D	E
17 M	46.18 CM	30.86 M	10.82 M	17 CM

4 The chart below shows goals scored and conceded in a football season. Which team has best goal difference?

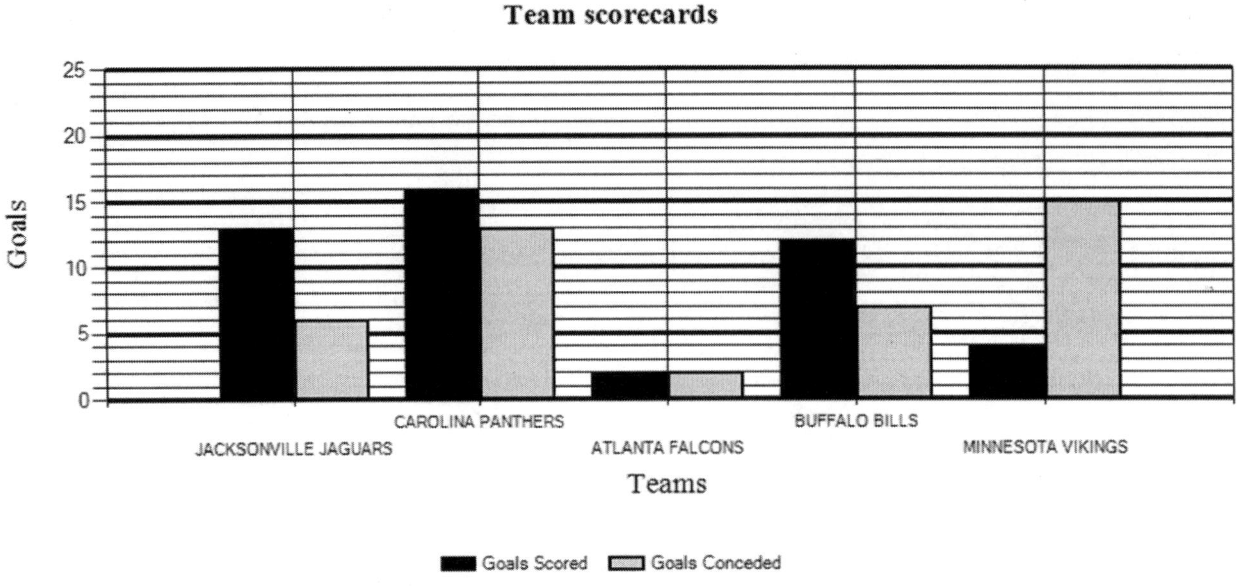

A	B	C	D	E
ATLANTA FALCONS	JACKSONVILLE JAGUARS	MINNESOTA VIKINGS	BUFFALO BILLS	CAROLINA PANTHERS

5 Look at the stack of cubes below. The stack is made of identical cubes. The volume of each individual cube is 3 cm^3. What is the total volume of the stack?

A	B	C	D	E
123 CM^3	241 CM^3	155 CM^3	247 CM^3	166 CM^3

 Published by Quattro Ethereal Ltd., PO Box 15794, Bromsgrove, B60 9GS, UK.

6 Which of the following letters has at least one line of symmetry?

J	N	A	P	S

A	B	C	D	E
J	N	A	P	S

7 Look at the shape below. The height of the rectangle is as shown in CM. If the perimeter of the rectangle is 54 CM, then what is the area of the shaded triangle in CM^2

A	B	C	D	E
92 sq cm	87 sq cm	89 sq cm	83 sq cm	88 sq cm

8 The tally chart below shows the chocolate preferred by students in a school. Each symbol represents 30 students ($ = 30 students)

GALAXY CARAMEL	$ $ $
MINSTRELS	$
MINI EGGS	$ $ $ $ $
MINT AERO	$ $ $
SMARTIES	$ $ $ $ $ $
CARAMAC	$ $ $ $ $ $
TERRYS CHOCOLATE	$ $ $ $
DAIRY MILK	$ $ $ $ $ $ $ $ $ $
TWIRL	$ $ $ $ $ $ $

How many students prefer Galaxy Caramels?

A	B	C	D	E
270	60	90	120	150

9 The graph below shows the results of a long jump competition at a local school in centimetres (cm). How much further did the winner of the competition jump as compared to the student who came last?

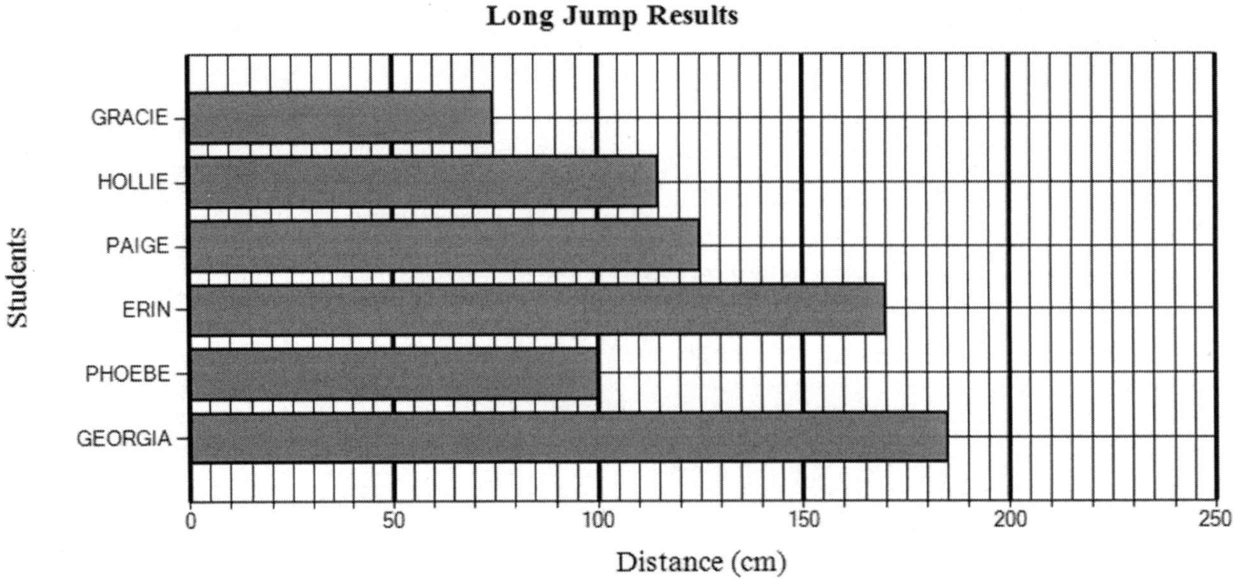

A	B	C	D	E
109 CM	122 CM	102 CM	96 CM	110 CM

10 Bethany is travelling from Bamako (Mali) to Praia (Cape Verde) in an airplane. The distance between the cities is 1712 Kilometres and the flying time is 2 hours and 30 minutes. The time in Praia is 1 hours and 0 minutes behind Bamako. The flight takes off at its scheduled time of 4:00AM and lands on time. Which of the following figures shows the local time in Praia when the flight lands?

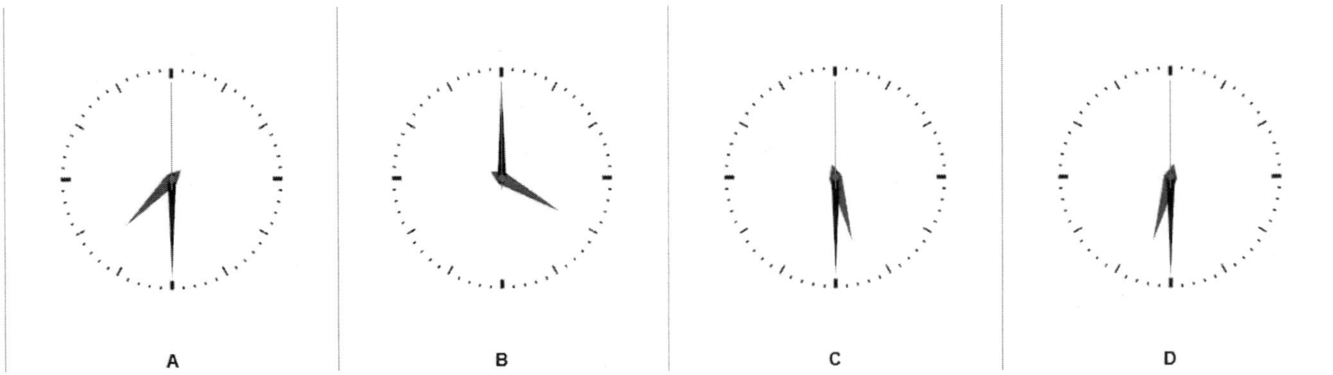

A	B	C	D	E
A	B	C	D	NONE

11 What will the co-ordinates of the marked point be on the grid if it moves LEFT by 1? (Note the origin of the grid).

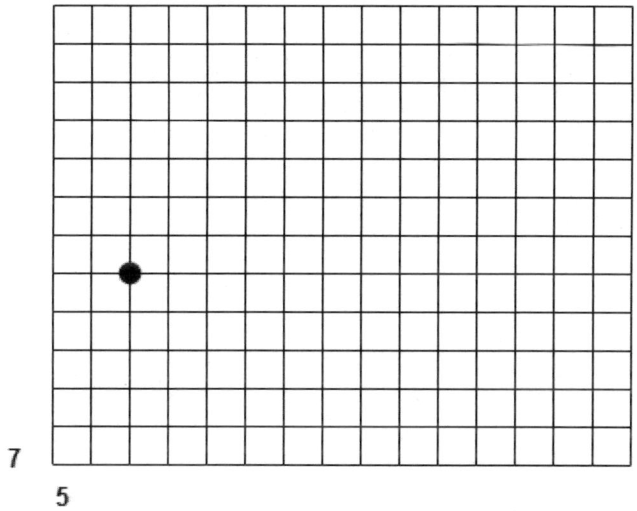

A	B	C	D	E
(6,12)	(12,10)	(13,11)	(14,8)	(16,8)

12 In the rectangle below, the ratio of HEIGHT to WIDTH is 7:14. If the HEIGHT is 2 metres, then what is the WIDTH?

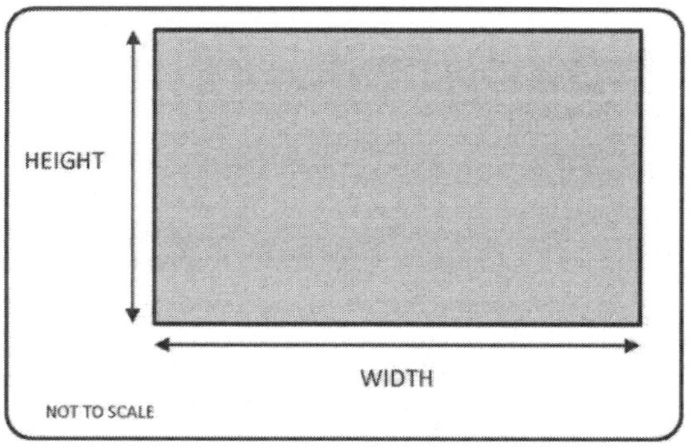

A	B	C	D	E
21	17	22	11	4

13 What percentage of the figure below is shaded

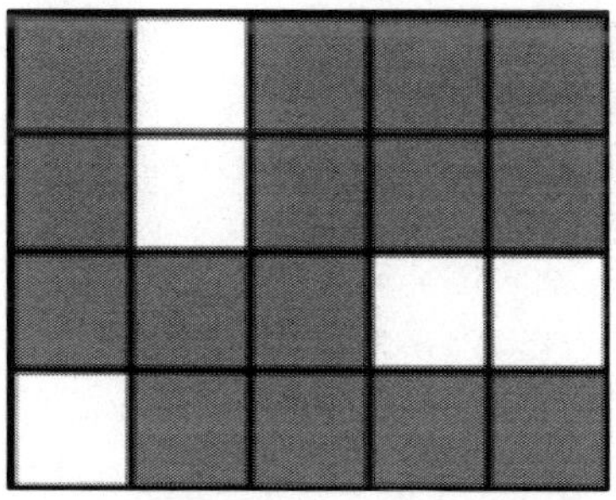

A	B	C	D	E
73.69%	75.00%	75.74%	73.86%	73.21%

14 Bingo balls shown below are placed in a bag. Tilly takes out one ball out at random. What is the probability that the ball is an even number or a number divisible by 5? Give your answer in its lowest terms.

A	B	C	D	E
1/5	3/7	1/3	4/11	5/13

15 Whilst playing scrabble Rosie is trying to create the word 'MEDICAL' and it is her turn to select a random letter from the bag.The letters available in the bag are shown below. If Rosie picks a random letter from the bag then what is the probability that it is a letter from the word 'MEDICAL'? Give your answer in its lowest terms.

A	B	C	D	E
3/8	2/5	3/10	2/11	1/11

16 The pie chart shows the proportions of different chocolates sold from a vending machine in one day. There were 88 BUTTONS sold. How many MARS were sold?

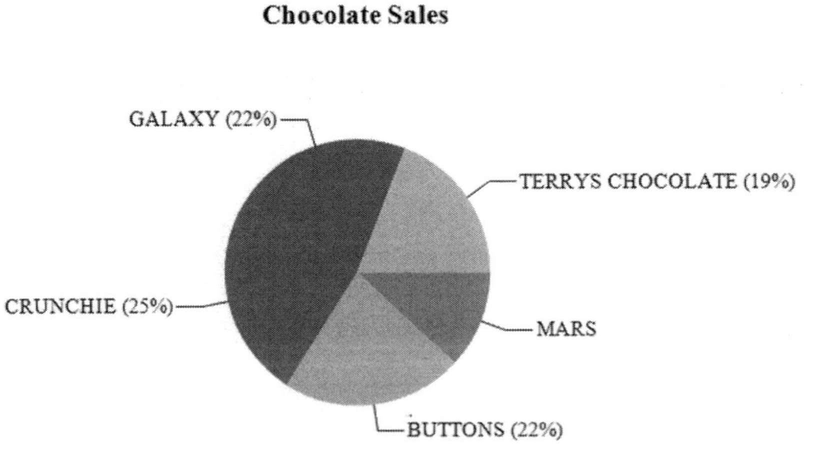

A	B	C	D	E
54	49	48	57	44

17 A comic costs 23 pence more than a book. If Four books and Five comics cost £3.22, then what is the price of a comic?

A	B	C	D	E
£0.46	£0.21	£0.40	£0.53	£0.78

18 ELLIE selected one of the spinners from the ones shown below. The selected spinner landed on an ODD number each time in a HUNDRED tries. Which spinner do you think ELLIE selected?

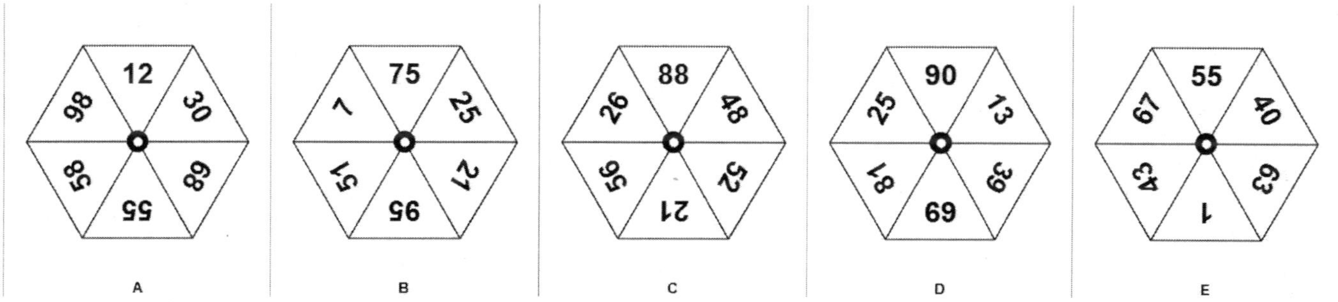

A	B	C	D	E
A	B	C	D	E

19 While on a holiday to SAUDI ARABIA, ANNA purchased a toy for 27 SAUDI RIYAL. The exchange rate is £1 = 6.11 SAUDI RIYAL. What is the cost of the toy in UK pounds?

A	B	C	D	E
£1.42	£1.66	£2.63	£1.24	£4.42

20 At CHLOE's school there are 220 students. 40% like FOOTBALL. How many students do not like FOOTBALL?

A	B	C	D	E
132	118	98	93	116

21 Look at two cuboids shown below. The dimensions of both the cuboids are shown in centimetres. What is the maximum number of smaller cuboids that you can fit inside the larger cuboid?

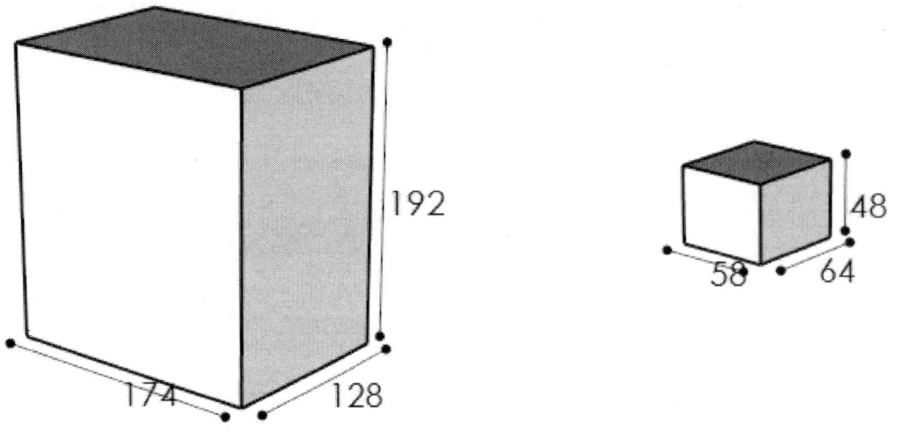

A	B	C	D	E
57	29	24	37	38

22 Which of the following fractions is the LARGEST?

A	B	C	D	E
3/4	2/5	16/25	5/4	7/50

23 The table below shows the number of drink cans sold from a vending machine on each day of the week. If the average sale per day was 9, then how many cans were sold on Saturday?

Monday	17
Tuesday	4
Wednesday	10
Thursday	4
Friday	2
Saturday	?
Sunday	14

A	B	C	D	E
13	7	3	15	12

24 Select ONE prime number from the following options.

A	B	C	D	E
50	100	23	80	68

25 Which cube net shown below would make a cube with two shaded sides adjacent to each other?

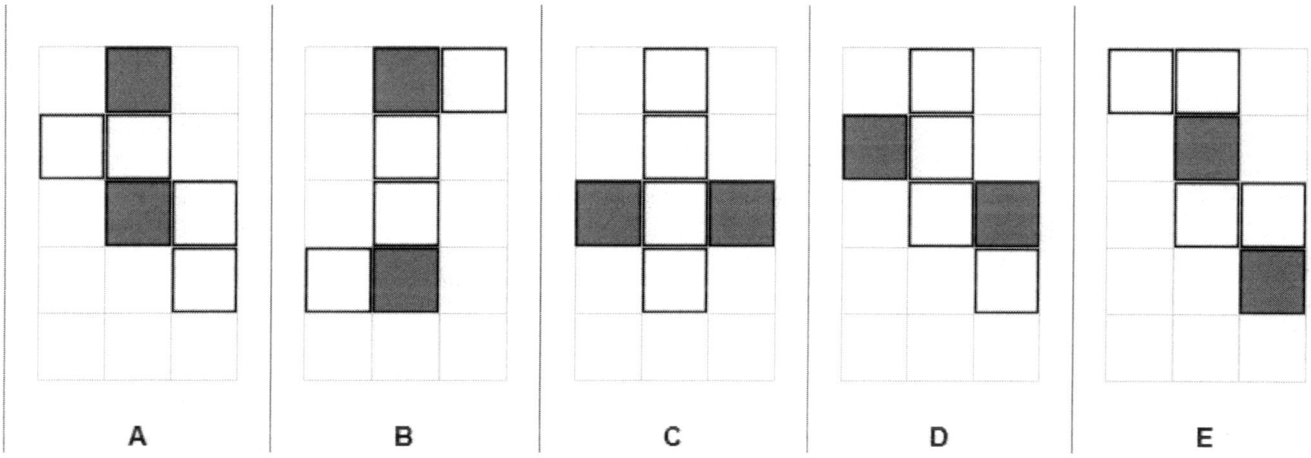

A	B	C	D	E
A	B	C	D	E

26 Look at the fraction below and fill in the missing number.

$$\frac{1}{3} \times \frac{5}{19} = \frac{5}{[\ \ ]}$$

A	B	C	D	E
46	57	50	65	23

27 The table below shows the prices of sweets at a shop. JULIA has £10.00 to do the shopping. If JULIA buys 6 LACES and 6 SOFT MINTS then how much money is JULIA left with?

TUTIE FRUITIES	64 pence
MOAMS	58 pence
SOFT MINTS	70 pence
LACES	59 pence
FLAKE	39 pence

A	B	C	D	E
£2.24	£1.12	£2.26	£2.30	£3.10

28 In the number machine shown below if X = 3 and Y = 343 then what number was put into the machine to start with?

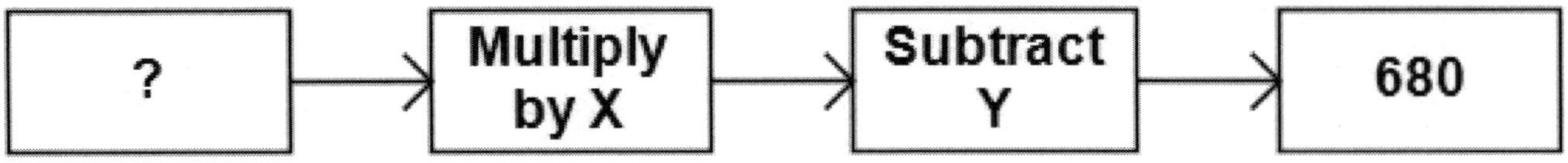

A	B	C	D	E
346	345	348	340	341

29 The village fete has a lucky dip where you are allowed to pick one of the treats in the box. The table below shows the mix of treats in the lucky dip box. What is the probability of picking JELLY BEANS from the dip?

MARS	11
ROLOS	23
BUTTONS	16
JELLY BEANS	22
IMPEREAL MINTS	5

A	B	C	D	E
1/12	1/6	16/63	23/86	2/7

30 A and B are two pulleys connected by a belt in a flour mill. For every SEVEN complete turns pulley A makes, pulley B makes FOURTEEN complete turns. If pulley A makes THIRTY NINE turns, then how many turns will pulley B make?

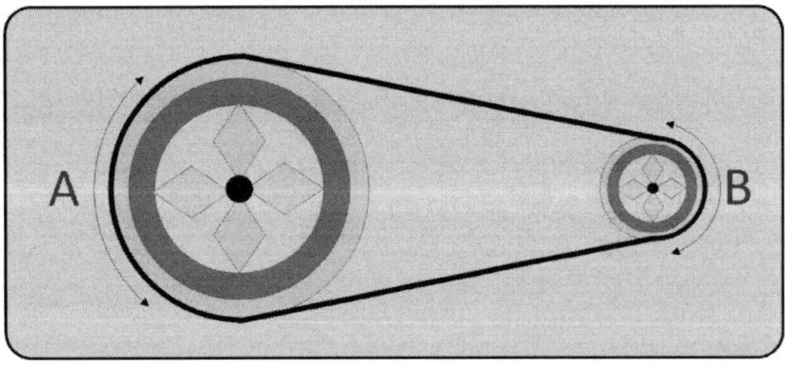

A	B	C	D	E
73	76	61	95	78

GO TO NEXT PAGE

PART 2

VERBAL REASONING - 15 MINUTES (26 QUESTIONS)

Section 1 - Cloze (8 Questions)

Complete the sentence by selecting one word from the options A-E. Mark your answer on the answer sheet.

31 Hush! [__________] come all the animals! The buffaloes, the blue deer, the red deer, the wild pigs, the hyenas, the wolves, the red dogs, and many others.

A	B	C	D	E
HERE	HAIR	HARE	HAIL	WHERE

32 See the buffaloes! They come after the elephants. But they do not come one behind another in a line, like the elephants. They come three or four together. They have beaten down the bushes to make a path and it is wide [_________] for three or four of them.

A	B	C	D	E
ROUGH	TROUGH	TOUGH	ENOUGH	BROOK

33 But why [_________] they drink three or four at the same time? Because the buffaloes are like a body of soldiers, one row behind another. Sometimes twenty or thirty rows make up a herd. We see only the first row drinking at a time.

A	B	C	D	E
WHERE	QUESTION	MUST	WATER	MUSK

34 But now let us watch the first row drinking. They are all bull buffaloes, the Papas of the herd. You can tell that by their huge horns, a yard long on each [_________] of the head. You see how the buffaloes stand side by side, so that their horns almost touch one another.

A	B	C	D	E
BESIDE	BEDSIDE	SALE	SIDE	SOLE

35 The narrow passage ended in a round arch all fringed with ferns and creepers. They [_______] through the arch into a deep, narrow gully whose banks were of stones, moss-covered; and in the crannies grew more ferns and long grasses.

A	B	C	D	E
PLAUSE	APPLAUSE	PASSING	PASSED	PROSE

36 Then came a [______] of daylight that grew and grew, and looked out over a scene so like a picture out of a book about Italy that everyone's breath was taken away, and they simply stood there staring.

A	B	C	D	E
GRIMMER	GRIME	GAME	MIRROR	GLIMMER

37 But they did not meet anybody else, and the scary feeling got thicker and thicker, till they were almost afraid of the sound of their feet on the gravel path. [______] the rose garden was a hedge with an arch cut in it, and it was the beginning of a maze like the one in Hampton Court.

A	B	C	D	E
YONDER	BEYOND	HORIZON	OBLIVION	THERE

38 He walked forward, winding the red thread round his fingers as he went. The path led them right into the [______] of the maze. And in the very middle of the maze they came upon the secret.

A	B	C	D	E
MIDDLE	UNDER	BESIDES	OVER	LEFT

Section 2 – Synonyms (12 Questions)

Select the word closest in meaning to the word given below. Mark your answer from the options A-E on the answer sheet.

39 DILEMMA

A	B	C	D	E
PROBABLY	PLURAL	PROBLEM	PECULIAR	PITY

40 LATTER

A	B	C	D	E
LATELY	FIRST	SECOND	LITTER	END

41 UMPIRE

A	B	C	D	E
REASON	RULES	ENFORCER	REFEREE	REGAL

42 BENCHMARK

A	B	C	D	E
QUALITY	TIDEMARK	STABLE	CHAIR	REFERENCE

43 FLUENT

A	B	C	D	E
FLOW	LANGUAGE	SPEAKER	SMOOTHIE	SMOOTHLY

44 SCHEDULE

A	B	C	D	E
TIME	TIMETABLE	TIDE	TABLE	TAPE

45 ANALOGY

A	B	C	D	E
DIGITAL	SIMILARITY	TWINS	TRIPLETS	ZOOLOGY

46 QUIRKY

A	B	C	D	E
CLOWN	FUNNY	UNCOMMON	SIMPLE	MIDDLE

47 TANTRUM

A	B	C	D	E
OUTBURST	TUNE	TRICK	EXPLOSION	BURST

48 NOMINATE

A	B	C	D	E
ANOINT	APPOINT	OINTMENT	PIN	REPORT

49 SYNTHETIC

A	B	C	D	E
NATURAL	ORGANIC	ARTIFICIAL	MODIFIED	SAFE

50 OBSOLETE

A	B	C	D	E
LATE	LATELY	DREAD	EXPIRED	NEW

Section 3 - Shuffled Sentences (6 Questions)

The following sentences are shuffled. Select the word that needs to be removed so that you can re-arrange the rest of the words to make a sentence. Mark you answer on the answer sheet.

51 There was a book and pencil a on the many table.

A	B	C	D	E
WAS	BOOK	PENCIL	MANY	TABLE

52 The woman knows dropped her child in school went and shopping.

A	B	C	D	E
WOMAN	KNOWS	DROPPED	CHILD	SCHOOL

53 I got a call from cancel one of my old yesterday friends.

A	B	C	D	E
GOT	CALL	CANCEL	OLD	YESTERDAY

54 The girl not did finish her kind homework on time.

A	B	C	D	E
GIRL	FINISH	KIND	HOMEWORK	TIME

55 There was another something strange the about painting on the wall.

A	B	C	D	E
THERE	ANOTHER	SOMETHING	STRANGE	PAINTING

56 Gary lives in and London works in a clear bank.

A	B	C	D	E
LIVES	AND	LONDON	WORKS	CLEAR

GO TO NEXT PAGE

PART 3

NON VERBAL REASONING – 10 MINUTES (24 QUESTIONS)

Section 1 – 3D Plane View (6 Questions)

Work out which of the options is a bird's eye view (Plan View) of the 3D figure on the left.

57

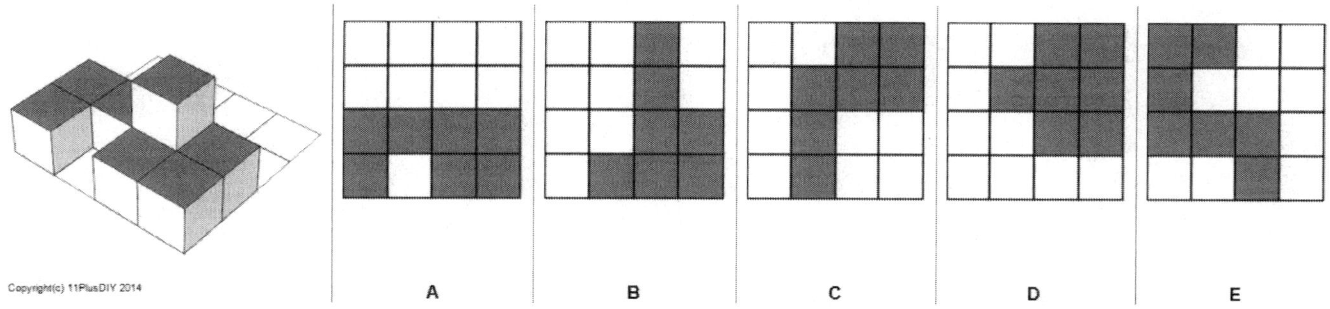

58

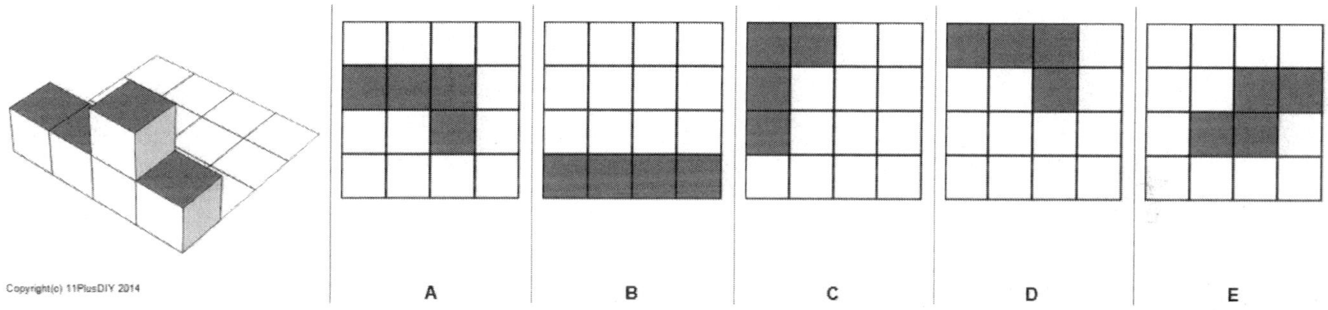

59

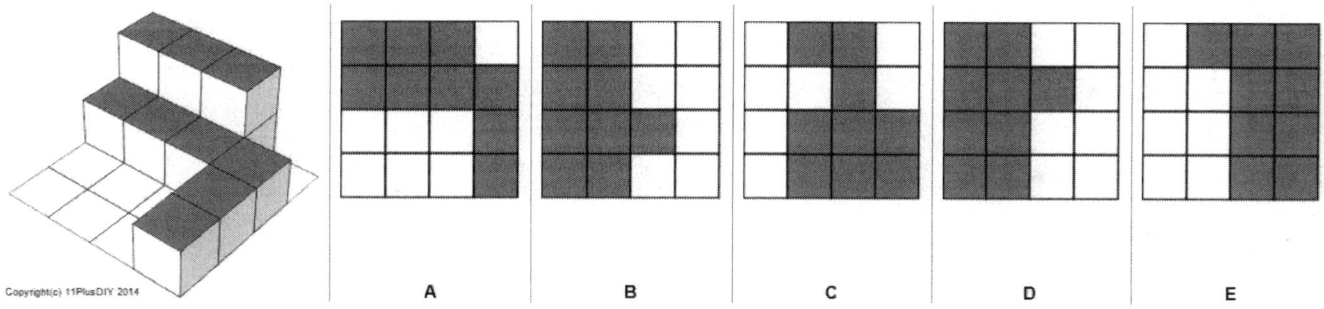

60

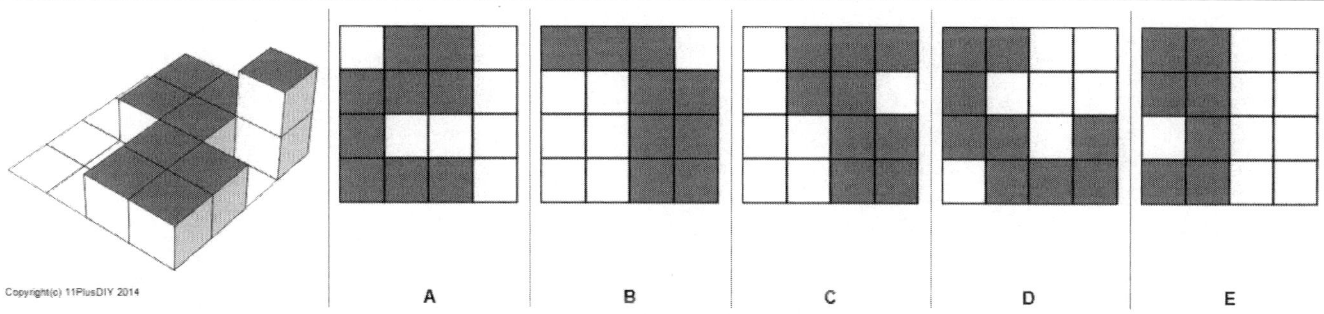

61

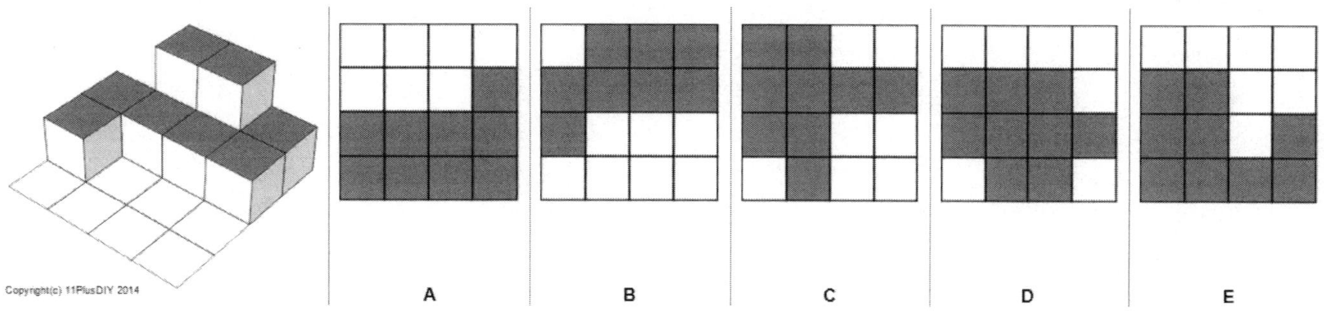

62

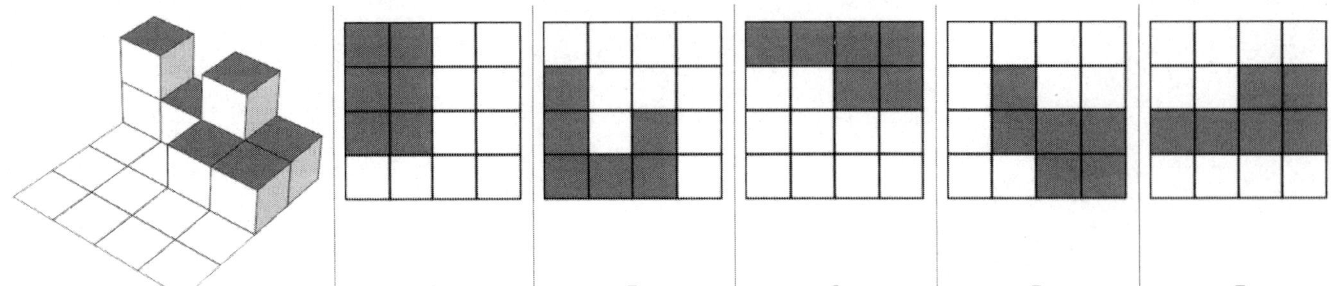

A B C D E

Section 2 – 3D Shape Rotation (6 Questions)

Select the shape from the options given which is a rotation of the shape on the left.

63

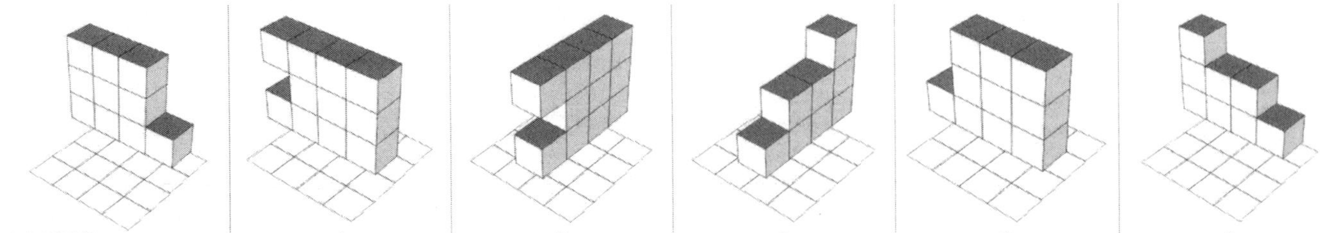

A B C D E

64

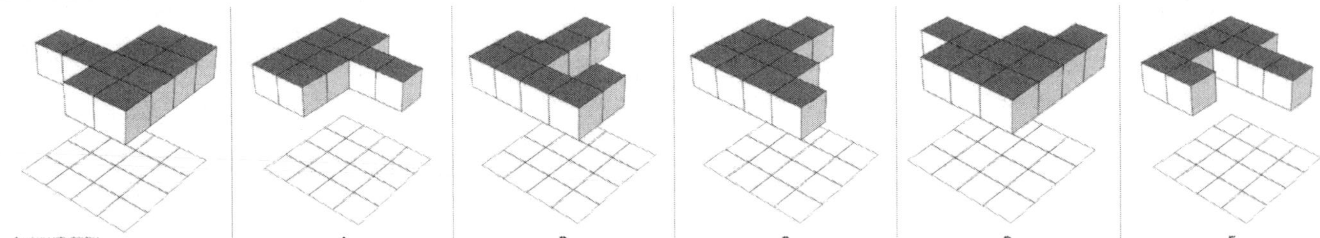

A B C D E

65

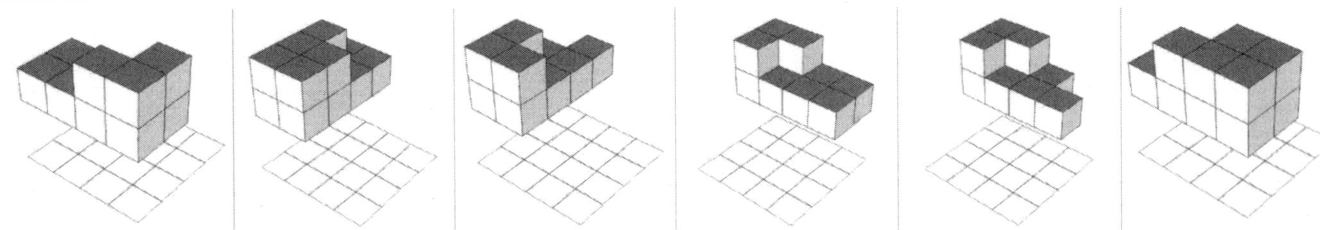

A B C D E

66

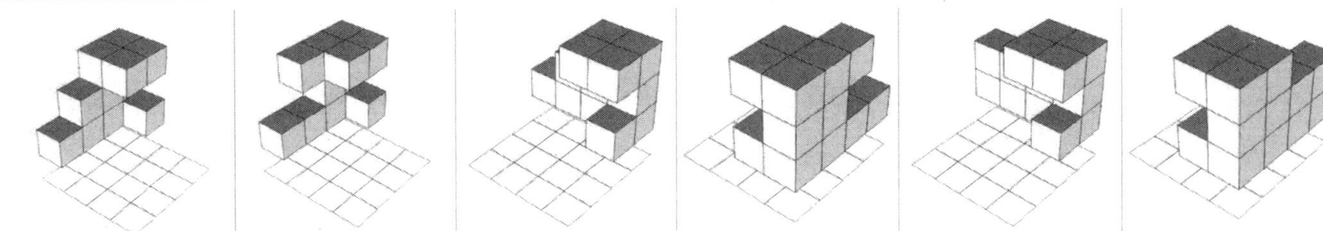

A B C D E

67

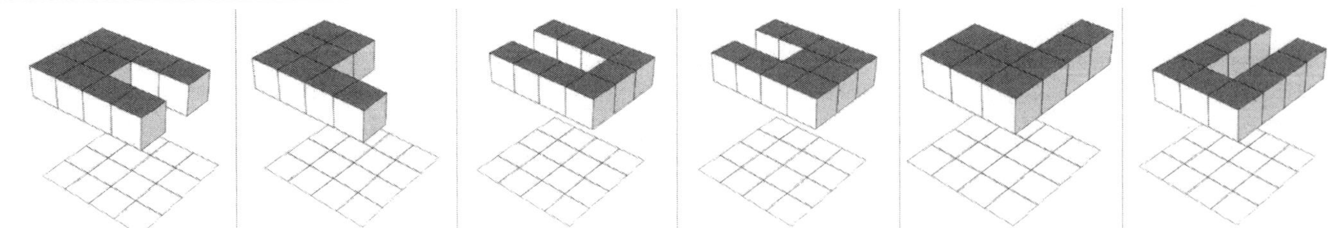

A B C D E

68

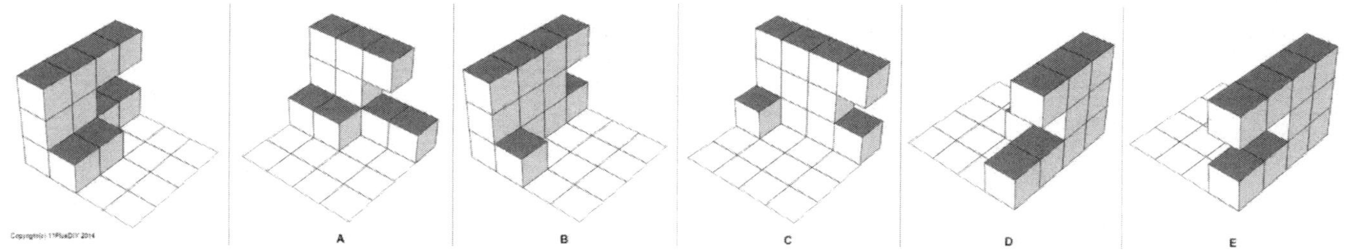

Section 3 - Simile (12 Questions)

Look at the two shapes separated by the words "is to" on the left. The first shape relates to the second one in some way. To the right of these shapes, there is a third shape followed by five other shapes. One of these given shapes is related to the third shape in the same way as the two shapes on the left are related to each other. Choose which one.

69

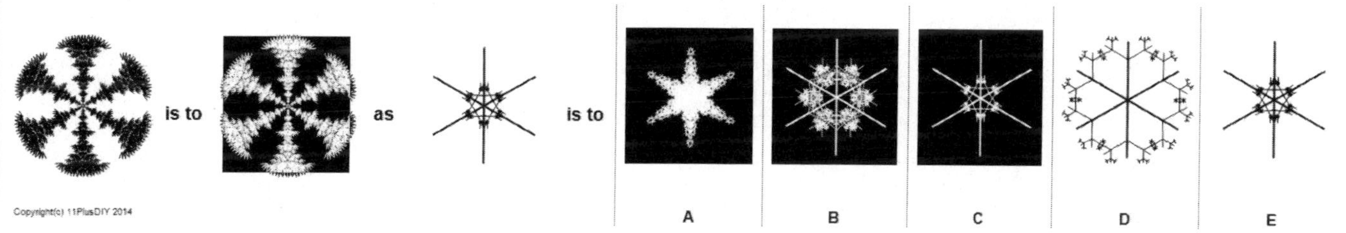

70

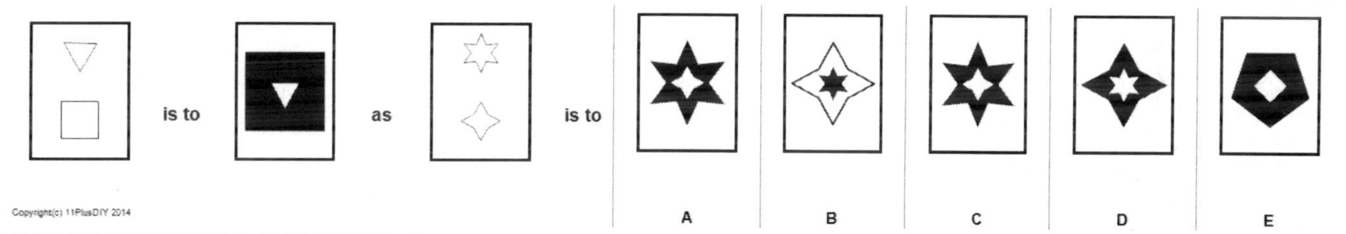

71

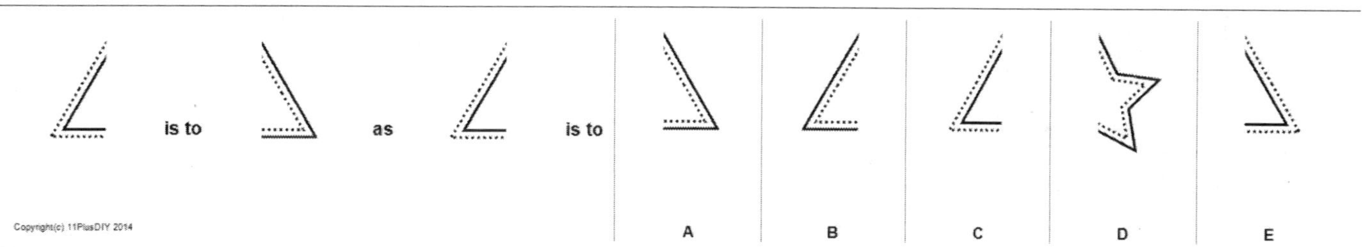

72

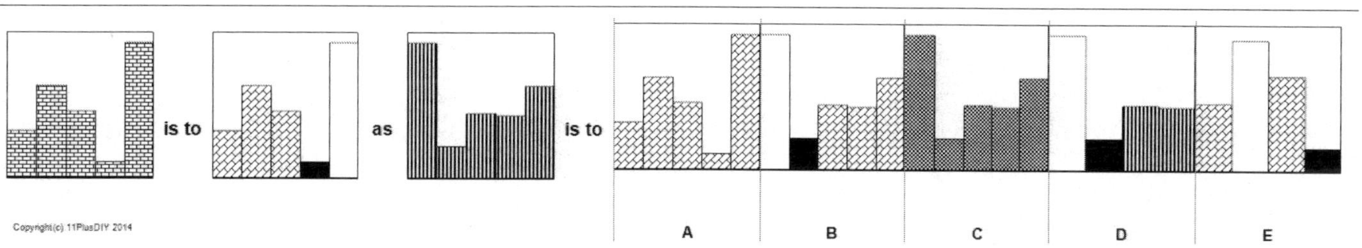

73

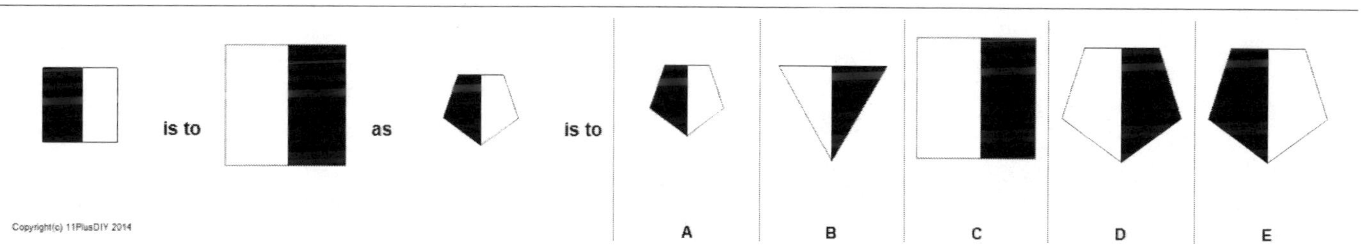

74

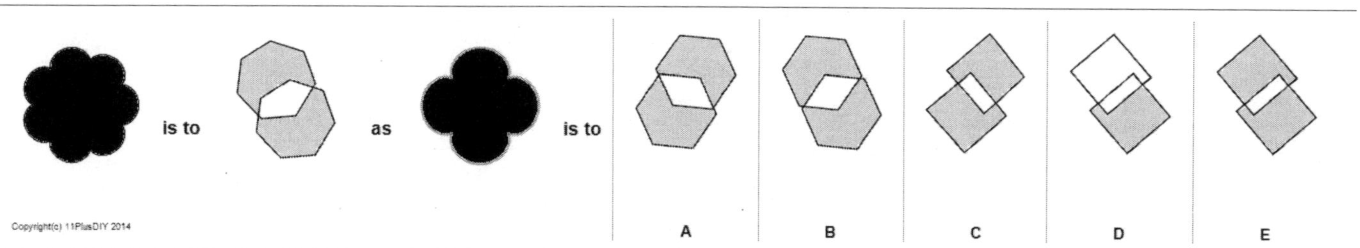

75

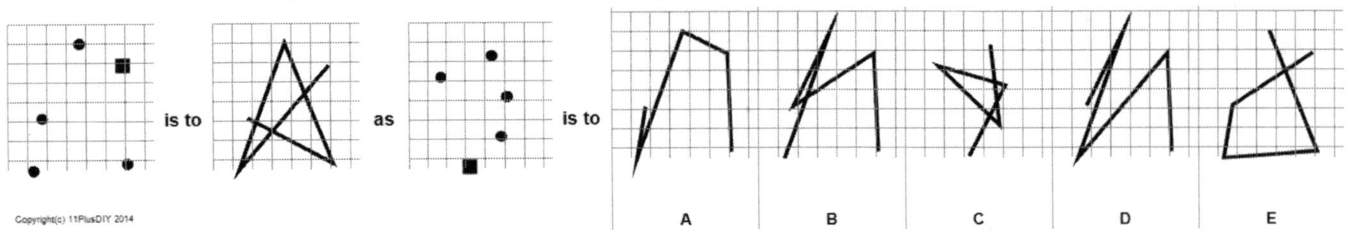

76

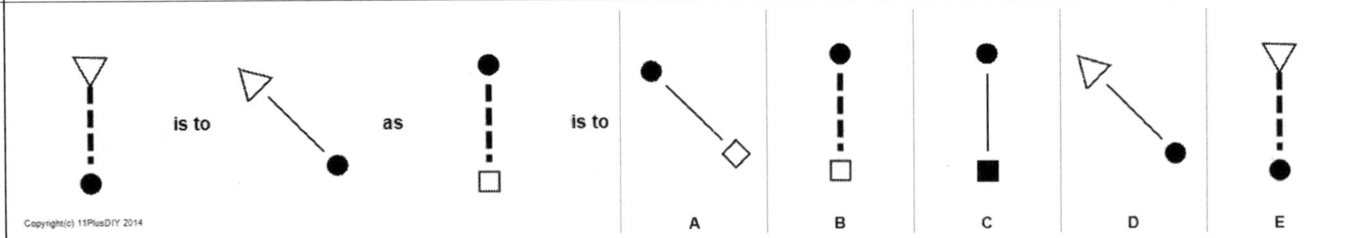

77

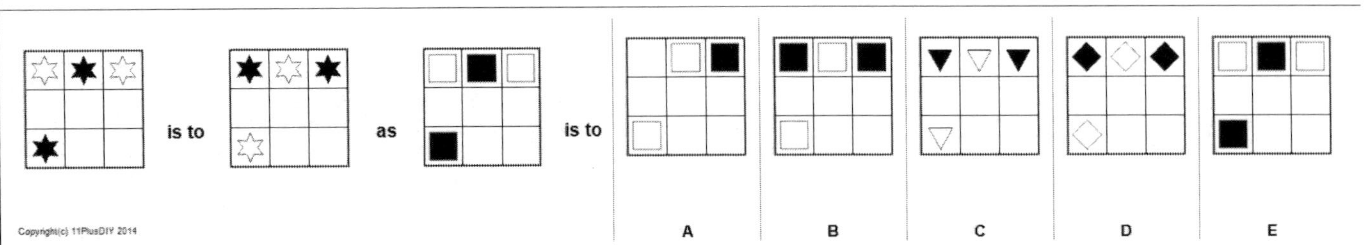

78

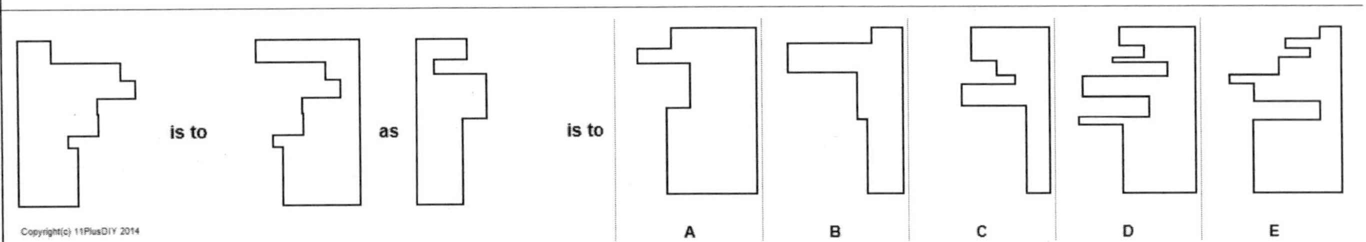

79

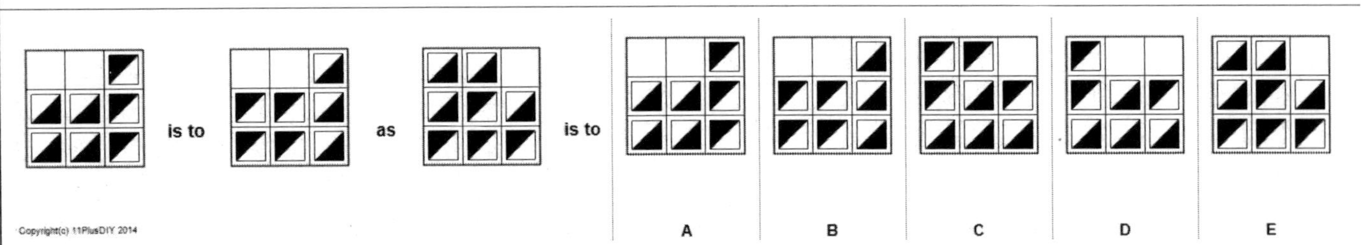

80

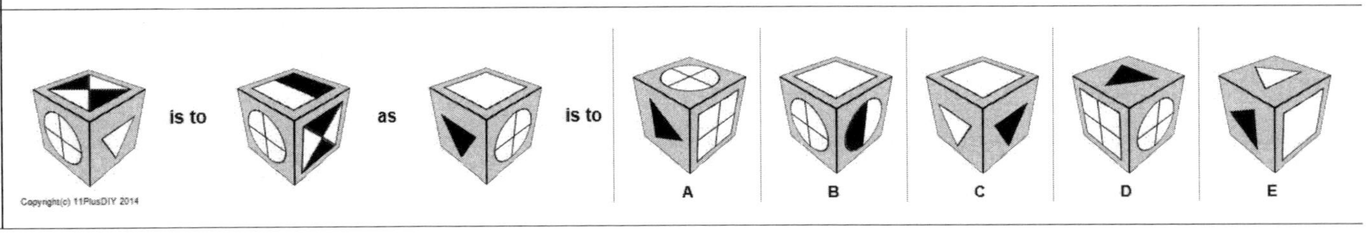

END OF TEST

11+ Mock Exam

MEC-15-001-B

Multiple-Choice Question Paper

Read the following carefully:

- There are three sections in this paper.
- You have 50 minutes in total to complete this paper. The time allowed for each section is given at the beginning of that section
- There are 80 questions in this paper and each question is worth 1 mark.
- You may work out the answers on a rough sheet of paper.
- The answers should be marked on the answer sheet provided as shown below. Do not mark your answers on the question paper.
- Make sure you mark the answer in the correct column matching the question number.
- If you make a mistake, rub out the answer completely before marking.
- You should only mark one answer for each question.
- If you find a question difficult, do not spend too much time on it. Move on to the next question and come back to it later.

80 Multiple Choice Questions to be completed in 50 minutes

QE Learning

www.QELearning.co.uk

PART 1

ENGLISH - 15 MINUTES (16 QUESTIONS)

Section 1 - Comprehension (16 Questions)

(Adapted from "Adapted from The Wind in the Willows", by Kenneth Grahame)

Read the passage below and answer the questions.

The Mole had been working very hard all morning, spring-cleaning his little home. First with brooms, then with dusters; then on ladders and steps and chairs, with a brush and a pail of whitewash; till he had dust in his throat and eyes, and splashes of whitewash all over his black fur, and an aching back and weary arms. It was small wonder, then, that he suddenly flung down his brush on the floor, and bolted out of the house without even waiting to put on his coat. Something up above was calling him imperiously, and he made for the steep little tunnel. So he scraped and scratched and scrabbled, working busily with his little paws and muttering to himself, "Up we go! Up we go!" till at last, "pop!" his snout came out into the sunlight, and he found himself rolling in the warm grass of a great meadow.

"This is fine!" he said to himself. "This is better than whitewashing!"

The sunshine struck hot on his fur, and the carol of happy birds fell on his dulled hearing almost like a shout. Jumping off all his four legs at once, in the joy of living and the delight of spring without its cleaning, he pursued his way across the meadow till he reached the hedge on the further side.

He thought his happiness was complete when, as he meandered aimlessly along, suddenly he stood by the edge of a full-fed river. Never in his life had he seen a river before--this sleek, sinuous, full-bodied animal, chasing and chuckling, gripping things with a gurgle and leaving them with a laugh. The Mole was fascinated.

As he sat on the grass and looked across the river, a dark hole in the bank opposite, just above the water's edge, caught his eye. As he gazed, something bright and small seemed to twinkle down in the heart of it, vanished, then twinkled once more like a tiny star. But it could hardly be a star in such an unlikely situation; and it was too glittering and small for a glow-worm. Then, as he looked, it winked at him, and so declared itself to be an eye; and a small face began gradually to grow up round it, like a frame round a picture. A brown little face, with whiskers. Small neat ears and thick silky hair. It was the Water Rat!

Then the two animals stood and regarded each other cautiously.

"Hello, Mole!" said the Water Rat.

"Hello, Rat!" said the Mole.

"Would you like to come over?" enquired the Rat presently.

"Oh, it's all very well to TALK," said the Mole, rather pettishly, being new to a river and riverside life and its ways.

The Rat said nothing, but stooped and unfastened a rope and hauled on it; then lightly stepped into a little boat which the Mole had not observed. It was painted blue outside and white within, and was just the size for two animals; and the Mole's whole heart went out to it at once, even though he did not yet fully understand its uses.

Then the Rat held up his forepaw as the Mole stepped gingerly down.

"Lean on that!" he said. "Now then, step lively!" and the Mole to his surprise and rapture found himself actually seated in the stern of a real boat.

"This has been a wonderful day! Do you know, I've never been in a boat before in all my life", he said.

"What?" cried the Rat, open-mouthed: "Never been in a--you never—well I--what have you been doing, then?"

The Rat brought the boat alongside the bank, made it fast, helped the still awkward Mole safely ashore, and swung out a luncheon-basket. The Mole begged as a favour to be allowed to unpack it all by himself; and the Rat was very pleased to indulge him, and to sprawl at full length on the grass and rest, while his excited friend shook out the table-cloth and spread it, took out all the mysterious packets one by one and arranged their contents in due order, still gasping, "O my! O my!" at each fresh revelation. When all was ready, the Rat said, "Now, pitch in, old fellow!" and the Mole was indeed very glad to obey, for he had started his spring-cleaning at a very early hour that morning, as people WILL do, and had not paused for a bite.

"What are you looking at?" said the Rat presently, when the edge of their hunger was somewhat dulled.

"I am looking," said the Mole, "at a streak of bubbles that I see travelling along the surface of the water. That is a thing that strikes me as funny."

"Bubbles? Oho!" said the Rat, and chirruped cheerily in an inviting sort of way.

A broad glistening muzzle showed itself above the edge of the bank, and the Otter hauled himself out and shook the water from his coat.

"Greedy beggars!" he observed, "Why didn't you invite me, Ratty?"

"This was an impromptu affair," explained the Rat. "By the way—my friend Mr. Mole."

"Proud, I'm sure," said the Otter, and the two animals were friends.

"All the world seems out on the river today", continued the Otter, "I came up this backwater to try and get a moment's peace, and then stumble upon you fellows!--At least--I beg pardon--I don't exactly mean that, you know."

---

1 What colour is the Mole?

A. Grey
B. Black
C. Red
D. Brown
E. Black and white.

2	Why did the Mole throw away the brush and leave his hole? A. He grew tired of cleaning his house and wanted some fresh air. B. He had to meet his friend, the Rat. C. He got angry because the brush left white marks on the floor. D. He heard a noise outside and wanted to find its source. E. He had to meet his friend, the Otter.
3	Which word is similar in meaning to "scrabbled", in line 7? A. "sneezed" B. "scrambled" C. "rushed" D. "slid" E. "dug"
4	Which do you think is the loudest sound the Mole hears before reaching the river? A. The twitter of the birds. B. The buzz of bees. C. The barking of dogs D. The gust of the wind E. The Mole cannot hear anything.
5	How many times does the Water Rat's eye twinkle? A. Once B. Three times C. Twice D. None at all E. Many times
6	What is the most fascinating aspect of the river, in the Mole's opinion? A. The sound of the rushing water impresses him most. B. The constant ripple of the water seems like a game to him. C. The colour of the water, mirroring the sunlight. D. The endless flow of water in all seasons appeals to him most. E. A. and B.
7	Which word has the opposite meaning to "pettishly", in line 30? A. "happy" B. "vexed" C. "grumpy" D. "crabby" E. "annoyed"

8 How do you explain the Mole's reaction to the Water Rat's invitation to approach the river?

A. He is afraid of the Water Rat.
B. He is cautious about the river because he has never seen it before.
C. He cannot swim as well as the Water Rat.
D. He feels too tired and wants to be alone.
E. He is afraid of Otters.

9 How does the Mole feel about the boat?

A. He likes the colours of the boat.
B. He is interested in the lunch basket.
C. He is indifferent to it, because he cannot see very well.
D. He likes it the moment he sees it.
E. He does not like it at all.

10 How does the Water Rat behave toward his new friend?

A. The Water Rat encourages the Mole to jump into the boat.
B. The Water Rat helps the Mole step into the boat.
C. The Water Rat laughs at the Mole's cautious moves.
D. The Water Rat helps the Mole open the lunch basket.
E. The Water Rat pushes the Mole into the boat.

11 What type of word is "unpack" in line 45?

A. Verb
B. Adjective
C. Pronoun
D. Adverb
E. Noun

12 What does the Rat's response in line 41 express?

A. anger
B. surprise
C. fear
D. threat
E. warning

13 Who opens the lunch basket first?

A. The Otter
B. The Mole
C. The Water Rat
D. It is open when they find it in the boat.
E. They leave it closed.

14 How does the Rat justify the fact that he has not invited the Otter to have lunch with him and the Mole?

A. He argues that there is not enough food in the basket.
B. He says he could not find the Otter all morning.
C. He says all the food belongs to the Mole.
D. He says they have not planned to have lunch.
E. He argues that there is no need of an invitation for friends.

15 Which word is similar in meaning to "stumble upon", in line 62?

A. meet
B. swim
C. see
D. hear
E. touch

16 How do you think the Mole feels about the newly arrived Otter?

A. The Mole is scared of big water animals.
B. The Mole is surprised to see the Rat has many friends.
C. The Mole is upset because he has to share the food with the Otter.
D. The Mole is happy to make a new friend on the same day.
E. The Mole is cautious, as he cannot defend himself against enemies.

GO TO NEXT PAGE

PART 2

VERBAL REASONING – 15 MINUTES (26 QUESTIONS)

Section 1 – Antonyms (12 Questions)

Select the word opposite in meaning to the word given below. Mark your answer from the options A-E on the answer sheet.

17 DIVERSE

A	B	C	D	E
DIVERSITY	DIFFERENT	SINGULAR	SIMILE	SIMILAR

18 PECULIAR

A	B	C	D	E
ODD	ODDITY	PERPENDICULAR	NORMAL	NORMALITY

19 ABYSMAL

A	B	C	D	E
SUPERB	ABYSS	SORCERER	AWFUL	DREADFUL

20 GREGARIOUS

A	B	C	D	E
SOCIABLE	SHY	EXTROVERT	UNRESERVED	SOCIAL

21 STUBBORN

A	B	C	D	E
PERSISTENT	FLEXIBLE	TENACIOUS	DETERMINED	IMMOVABLE

22 PROXIMATE

A	B	C	D	E
NEARBY	CLOSE	ADJACENT	ADJOINING	DISTANT

23 PERENNIAL

A	B	C	D	E
RECURRENT	PERPETUAL	CONSTANT	LASTING	OCCASIONAL

24 BOYCOTT

A	B	C	D	E
REFUSE	EMBARGO	SHUN	PARTICIPATE	PROHIBIT

25 ATHEIST

A	B	C	D	E
NON-BELIEVER	DISBELIEVER	RELIGIOUS	AGNOSTIC	HUMANIST

26 STAUNCH

A	B	C	D	E
LOYAL	WAVERING	RELIABLE	DEPENDABLE	FIRM

27 VINDICATE

A	B	C	D	E
IMPLICATE	JUSTIFY	CLAIM	SUPPORT	DEFEND

28 FUTILE

A	B	C	D	E
USELESS	USEFUL	POINTLESS	FRUITLESS	VAIN

GO TO NEXT PAGE

Section 2 – Homonyms (8 Questions)

In each of the following sentences, there is a word missing. Complete each sentence by selecting one word from the options A-E which fits both the sentences. Shade your answer on the answer sheet.

29 Danny _____________ into his burger hungrily.

The poor boy pleaded for a little _____________ of chocolate from the boy on the road.

A	B	C	D	E
CLIMBED	BIT	FOOD	MORSEL	CUBE

30 Maggi had to _____________ the whims and fancies of her boss.

Antarctica is the home of the beautiful polar _____________.

A	B	C	D	E
TOLERATE	BEAR	TIGER	UNDERSTAND	DOG

31 Rosy _____________ the game on the television.

Rob had used a _____________ for cutting down the tree.

A	B	C	D	E
WATCHED	AXE	NAIL	SAW	UNDERSTOOD

32 The beautiful _____________ used on the window was bought by me.

The accident left the workers _____________ in one eye.

A	B	C	D	E
LAME	CURTAIN	GLASS	BLIND	NET

33 Emily bought a red _____________ for her mother.

The sun _____________ at 5:30am this morning.

A	B	C	D	E
RISE	TULIP	DRESS	COAT	ROSE

34 The _____________ of wood was used by the carpenter.

Anne lived in the third _____________ down the lane.

A	B	C	D	E
STREET	PIECE	LOG	APARTMENT	BLOCK

35 The aborigines used the _____________ and arrow as a weapon.

Sally wore a _____________ on her dress for the party.

A	B	C	D	E
TIE	HANKY	KNIFE	BOW	DAGGER

36 The carpenter asked his client to get a a nut and _____________ to fix up the chair.

The door had a massive _____________ for the security of the house.

A	B	C	D	E
KEY	CHAIN	BOLT	NAILS	LOCK

Section 3 – Compound Words (6 Questions)

In each of the following choose the word which makes a new compound word when added to the word given. Shade your answer on the answer sheet.

37 AS

A	B	C	D	E
IN	READ	SORTED	TED	TEN

38 IN

A	B	C	D	E
HABITAT	HABIT	BIT	BYTE	BOAT

39 BIT

A	B	C	D	E
ONE	TEN	TWO	TIP	TELL

40 MODE

A	B	C	D	E
ROW	ROAD	RAIL	RITE	RATE

41 GOVERN

A	B	C	D	E
AN	IN	OR	AS	OF

42 STAR

A	B	C	D	E
RIP	RAP	RAT	RED	RATE

GO TO NEXT PAGE

PART 3

MATHEMATICS - 20 MINUTES (38 QUESTIONS)

Section 1 - Short Maths (30 Questions).

43 What is 788 + 894?

A	B	C	D	E
1682	1680	1676	1675	1672

44 What is 10% of 300?

A	B	C	D	E
30	32	38	33	44

45 If 13x - 608 = -478, then what is the value of x?

A	B	C	D	E
15	22	24	13	10

46 What is 20:43 on the 12 hour clock?

A	B	C	D	E
02:43 AM	02:43 PM	08:43 PM	09:13 PM	08:43 AM

47 What is 35 x 18?

A	B	C	D	E
629	630	635	620	638

48 Which of the following is exactly divisible by 12?

A	B	C	D	E
1963	3074	384	2375	1208

49 How many minutes are there between 05:00 and 08:10?

A	B	C	D	E
182	43	250	142	190

50 How many vertices does a 3D-CONE have?

A	B	C	D	E
8	4	7	1	5

51 What is the difference between 60% of 900 and 40% of 600?

A	B	C	D	E
569	300	446	373	579

52 What is four fifths of 115?

A	B	C	D	E
92	47	98	144	116

53 Increase £13.00 by 40%.

A	B	C	D	E
£39.00	£32.00	£18.20	£38.00	£33.00

54 What sum of money multiplied by 19 equals £247.00?

A	B	C	D	E
£10.00	£13.00	£17.00	£16.00	£12.00

55 If 25% of a number is 400, then what is the number?

A	B	C	D	E
1600	2678	2744	3118	1951

56 Which of the following numbers are multiples of 7, 9 and 6?

A	B	C	D	E
216	252	203	293	215

57 What is the HCF (Highest Common Factor) of 69 and 45?

A	B	C	D	E
9	3	7	8	6

58 What is the value of 318 - 277?

A	B	C	D	E
31	44	46	41	37

59 What is the product of 21, 19 and 12?

A	B	C	D	E
4793	4788	4797	4785	4784

60 What is the LCM (Lowest Common Multiple) of 22 and 12?

A	B	C	D	E
132	97	69	16	52

61 Calculate the median of the following: 20, 75, 85, 2, 33, 16, 64, 71, 79

A	B	C	D	E
64	2	79	85	71

62 Calculate the range of the following: -78, 51, -3, 57, 64, 31, 79, -71, -16

A	B	C	D	E
51	157	-16	-71	31

63 Which of the following is an obtuse angle?

A	B	C	D	E
340	1	115	66	355

64 How many times greater is 546 than 21?

A	B	C	D	E
59	24	26	46	34

65 What is the difference in metres between 56.5 km and 25.2 km?

A	B	C	D	E
31300	51362	32448	24428	61098

66 What is the square root of 289?

A	B	C	D	E
38	41	21	24	17

67 What is the area of a square (in square cm) with sides measuring 16 cm?

A	B	C	D	E
256	385	285	347	192

68 What is the perimeter of a regular pentagon (in cm) with sides measuring 20 cm?

A	B	C	D	E
112	138	61	110	100

69 What is the product of 90 and 7.5?

A	B	C	D	E
675	999	1188	608	904

70 How many fives are there in 195?

A	B	C	D	E
47	39	6	42	28

71 Calculate the mode of the following numbers: 15,10,10,2,17,2,15,7,15,2,2

A	B	C	D	E
7	2	17	15	10

72 How many days are there in total in August and January?

A	B	C	D	E
66	94	76	29	62

GO TO NEXT PAGE

Section 2 - Long Maths (8 Questions).

73 A car travels for 1 hour 10 minutes at 60 kmph and then for 1 hour 30 minutes at 108 kmph. How far did it travel?

A	B	C	D	E
235 KM	243 KM	229 KM	232 KM	239 KM

74 A car takes 1 hours and 15 minutes to travel 165 km. What is its speed?

A	B	C	D	E
133 KMPH	130 KMPH	132 KMPH	123 KMPH	136 KMPH

75 Which of the following measures approximately 2 CENTIMETRES?

A	B	C	D	E
BED	KEY	TENNIS RACKET	POSTAGE STAMP	LCD TV

76 LOLA is making a BANOFFEE PIE from a recipe which is in imperial units. The recipe requires 12 oz of Butter. Assuming 1 oz = 30 gms and rounding to the nearest 5 gms, how much Butter should LOLA use?

A	B	C	D	E
535 G	210 G	445 G	360 G	220 G

77 The table below shows the temperatures recorded in cities around the world. Which city was the coldest?

YEREVAN	26 deg C
ABU DHABI	-6 deg C
SINGAPORE	14 deg C
ABUJA	-4 deg C
OTTAWA	-1 deg C

A	B	C	D	E
YEREVAN	ABU DHABI	SINGAPORE	ABUJA	OTTAWA

78 BROOKE is baking cup-cakes for charity. If each cup-cake requires 7 ml of vanilla essence and BROOKE has 105 ml of vanilla essence, the how many cup-cakes can BROOKE bake?

A	B	C	D	E
15	19	17	12	18

79 From a 6 metre length of ribbon I cut 192 centimetres and then 1.5 metres. How much ribbon is left?

A	B	C	D	E
2.58 M	2.76 M	6.88 M	5.87 M	4.74 M

80 Use the table below to convert 77 grams into ounces

30 gms	1.06 ounces
25 gms	0.88 ounces
49 gms	1.73 ounces
15 gms	0.53 ounces
32 gms	1.13 ounces
59 gms	2.08 ounces

A	B	C	D	E
3.89 OZ	2.72 OZ	1.74 OZ	4.94 OZ	2.96 OZ

END OF TEST

MEC-15-001-A

1	180 sq cm	C	10 x 18 = 180 sq cm
2	729 cm^2	A	Perimeter is 36 cm therefore each side is 9. Volume of the cube is 9 x 9 x 9 = 729 Cm^3
3	17 m	A	Length of first side is = Tile Side x No of tiles used = 10 x 41 The length of second side can be calculated by dividing the total tiles used by the number of tiles along one side. The two sides therefore are 410 and 440 cm
4	JACKSONVILLE JAGUARS	B	Best team has a goal difference of 7.
5	123 cm^3	A	Count the total number of cubes and multiply it by the volume of single cube.
6	A	C	
7	88 sq cm	E	If the perimeter is 54 cm then the base is 16 cm. The area is calculated as (base x altitude) ÷ 2 = 88 sq cm
8	90	C	Symbols x Multiple = 3 x 30 = 90
9	110 cm	E	Max = 185 cm. Min = 75 cm. The range = 185 - 75 = 110 cm.
10	C	C	
11	(6,12)	A	Count the grid along the X and Y axis. Also note the starting point of the grid.
12	4	E	(14 ÷ 7) x 2 = 4
13	75.00%	B	15 out of 20 = 75.00%
14	5/13	E	There are 3 balls which have numbers divisible by 5. There are 2 balls which have even numbers. The probability is therefore 5 / 13 = 5/13
15	2/11	D	There are 11 letters in the bag. Of these only 2 letters appear in the word 'MEDICAL'. The probability therefore = 2/11.
16	48	C	Calculate the percentage share of MARS. Quantity of MARS Sold = (88 ÷ 22) x 12
17	£0.46	A	(£0.23 x 4) + (£0.46 x 5) = £3.22
18	B	B	The answer is the spinner with only ODD numbers.
19	£4.42	E	Cost in Pounds = 27 ÷ 6.11 = £4.42
20	132	A	If 40% like FOOTBALL then 60% do not like FOOTBALL. 60% of total student population = 132
21	24	C	Calculate the volume of both the cubes and divide the volume of the larger cube by the volume of the smaller cube.
22	5/4	D	The fractions in ascending order are = 7/50 , 2/5 , 16/25 , 3/4 , 5/4
23	12	E	Total sales for the week excluding Saturday = 51. Therefore sale for Saturday = (9 x 7) - 51 = 12
24	23	C	23 is a prime number.
25	B	B	
26	57	B	
27	£2.26	C	Cost for 6 LACES = £3.54. Cost for 6 SOFT MINTS = £4.20. Total cost = £7.74
28	341	E	(341 x 3) - 343 = 680
29	2/7	E	22 / Sum of all chocolates = 22/77 = 2/7
30	78	E	(14 ÷ 7) x 39 = 78
31	HERE	A	
32	ENOUGH	D	
33	MUST	C	
34	SIDE	D	
35	PASSED	D	
36	GLIMMER	E	
37	BEYOND	B	
38	MIDDLE	A	
39	PROBLEM	C	
40	END	E	
41	REFEREE	D	
42	REFERENCE	E	
43	SMOOTHLY	E	
44	TIME TABLE	B	
45	SIMILARITY	B	
46	UNCOMMON	C	
47	OUTBURST	A	
48	APPOINT	B	
49	ARTIFICIAL	C	
50	EXPIRED	D	
51	MANY	D	There was a book and a pencil on the table.
52	knows	B	The woman dropped her child in school and went shopping.
53	cancel	C	I got a call from one of my old friends yesterday.
54	kind	C	The girl did not finish her homework on time.
55	another	B	There was something strange about the painting on the wall.
56	clear	E	Gary lives in London and works in a bank.
57	A	A	
58	B	B	
59	A	A	
60	C	C	
61	B	B	
62	C	C	
63	D	D	
64	A	A	
65	C	C	
66	B	B	
67	C	C	
68	E	E	
69	C	C	Inversed background on snowflake.

70	D	D	The small shapes on the top and bottom move to the centre. The shape at the bottom becomes larger. The bigger shape is shaded black.
71	A	A	Match the rest of the half shape. The line styles also change in the next step.
72	B	B	The tallest value of the histogram get shaded White and the smallest Black.
73	D	D	Match the increase or decrease in shape size and the half shaded.
74	E	E	The starting shape has 4 sides. The matching shape should also have the same number of sides. The new shape pair realign diagonally. Either the top, bottom or both parts of the new overlapping shape pair is shaded.
75	C	C	
76	A	A	Icons switch places. The line thickness toggles between thin and thick. The line style toggles between solid and dashed. Clockwise rotation by 135 degrees.
77	B	B	Shape polygons stay in the same cell in the grid, but toggle between black and white.
78	A	A	Lock and Key pairs. Match the teeth of the lock with the key.
79	C	C	The partial shading of the cells moves from Top-left to Bottom-right. The location stays the same.
80	E	E	Match cube rotation along X, Y or Z axis.

MEC-15-001-B			
1	B	B	
2	A	A	
3	E	E	
4	A	A	
5	C	C	
6	E	E	
7	A	A	
8	B	B	
9	D	D	
10	B	B	
11	A	A	
12	B	B	
13	B	B	
14	D	D	
15	A	A	
16	D	D	
17	SIMILAR	E	
18	NORMAL	D	
19	SUPERB	A	
20	SHY	B	
21	FLEXIBLE	B	
22	DISTANT	E	
23	OCCASIONAL	E	
24	PARTICIPATE	D	
25	RELIGIOUS	C	
26	WAVERING	B	
27	IMPLICATE	A	
28	USEFUL	B	
29	BIT	B	
30	BEAR	B	
31	SAW	D	
32	BLIND	D	
33	ROSE	E	
34	BLOCK	E	
35	BOW	D	
36	BOLT	C	
37	SORTED	C	ASSORTED
38	HABIT	B	INHABIT
39	TEN	B	BITTEN
40	RATE	E	MODERATE
41	OR	C	GOVERNOR
42	RED	D	STARRED
43	1682	A	788 + 894 = 1682
44	30	A	10% of 300 is 30
45	10	E	(13 x 10) - 608 = -478
46	08:43 PM	C	
47	630	B	35 x 18 = 630
48	384	C	Divide each option by 12
49	190	E	
50	1	D	3D-CONE has 1 vertices.
51	300	B	60% of 900 is 540. 40% of 600 is 240
52	92	A	(4/5)115 = 92
53	£18.20	C	40% of £13.00 is £5.20
54	£13.00	B	19 times £13.00 is £247.00
55	1600	A	25% of 1600 is 400.
56	252	B	7, 9 and 6 are all factors of 252.

57	3	B	Factors of 69 are 1, 3, 23. Factors of 45 are 1, 3, 5, 9, 15.
58	41	D	318 - 277 = 41
59	4788	B	21 x 19 x 12 = 4788
60	132	A	Factors of 22 are 1, 2, 11. Factors of 12 are 1, 2, 3, 4, 6
61	64	A	The value in the middle when arranged in ascending order is 64
62	157	B	Maximum and Minimum values are 79 and -78. The range is (79 - -78) = 157
63	115	C	Obtuse angle is more than 90 and less than 180 degrees.
64	26	C	21 x 26 = 546
65	31300	A	(56.5 - 31300) x 1000 = 31300
66	17	E	17 x 17 = 289
67	256	A	16 x 16 = 256
68	100	E	20 x 5 = 100 cm
69	675	A	90 x 7.5 = 675
70	39	B	(1/5)195 = 39
71	2	B	The number 2 appears maximum times in the series.
72	62	E	31 + 31 = 62
73	232 km	D	Distance = Speed × Time.
74	132 kmph	C	Speed = Distance ÷ Time.
75	POSTAGE STAMP	D	
76	360g	D	1 oz = 30 gms, therefore 12 Oz = 12 x 30 = 360g gms
77	ABU DHABI	B	-6 was the lowest temperature
78	15	A	The essence needed for 15 cakes = 7 x 15 = 105 ml. The remainder is 0 ml.
79	2.58 m	A	6 - (1.92 + 1.5) = 2.58 m
80	2.72 oz	B	Add the table entries for 15, 32 and 30 g.

Pupil ID

Pupil Name

Date of Birth

Venue

- Check that you are marking the answer for the correct question number.
- Shade ONE answer only unless specified.
- Use an HB pencil and rub out any errors thoroughly.
- Shade boxes like this: B

1 A B C D E	2 A B C D E	3 A B C D E	4 A B C D E	5 A B C D E	6 A B C D E	7 A B C D E	8 A B C D E	9 A B C D E	10 A B C D E
11 A B C D E	12 A B C D E	13 A B C D E	14 A B C D E	15 A B C D E	16 A B C D E	17 A B C D E	18 A B C D E	19 A B C D E	20 A B C D E
21 A B C D E	22 A B C D E	23 A B C D E	24 A B C D E	25 A B C D E	26 A B C D E	27 A B C D E	28 A B C D E	29 A B C D E	30 A B C D E
31 A B C D E	32 A B C D E	33 A B C D E	34 A B C D E	35 A B C D E	36 A B C D E	37 A B C D E	38 A B C D E	39 A B C D E	40 A B C D E
41 A B C D E	42 A B C D E	43 A B C D E	44 A B C D E	45 A B C D E	46 A B C D E	47 A B C D E	48 A B C D E	49 A B C D E	50 A B C D E
51 A B C D E	52 A B C D E	53 A B C D E	54 A B C D E	55 A B C D E	56 A B C D E	57 A B C D E	58 A B C D E	59 A B C D E	60 A B C D E
61 A B C D E	62 A B C D E	63 A B C D E	64 A B C D E	65 A B C D E	66 A B C D E	67 A B C D E	68 A B C D E	69 A B C D E	70 A B C D E
71 A B C D E	72 A B C D E	73 A B C D E	74 A B C D E	75 A B C D E	76 A B C D E	77 A B C D E	78 A B C D E	79 A B C D E	80 A B C D E

Pupil ID

Pupil Name

Date of Birth

Venue

- Check that you are marking the answer for the correct question number.
- Shade ONE answer only unless specified.
- Use an HB pencil and rub out any errors thoroughly.
- Shade boxes like this: D

1	2	3	4	5	6	7	8	9	10
A	A	A	A	A	A	A	A	A	A
B	B	B	B	B	B	B	B	B	B
C	C	C	C	C	C	C	C	C	C
D	D	D	D	D	D	D	D	D	D
E	E	E	E	E	E	E	E	E	E

11	12	13	14	15	16	17	18	19	20
A	A	A	A	A	A	A	A	A	A
B	B	B	B	B	B	B	B	B	B
C	C	C	C	C	C	C	C	C	C
D	D	D	D	D	D	D	D	D	D
E	E	E	E	E	E	E	E	E	E

21	22	23	24	25	26	27	28	29	30
A	A	A	A	A	A	A	A	A	A
B	B	B	B	B	B	B	B	B	B
C	C	C	C	C	C	C	C	C	C
D	D	D	D	D	D	D	D	D	D
E	E	E	E	E	E	E	E	E	E

31	32	33	34	35	36	37	38	39	40
A	A	A	A	A	A	A	A	A	A
B	B	B	B	B	B	B	B	B	B
C	C	C	C	C	C	C	C	C	C
D	D	D	D	D	D	D	D	D	D
E	E	E	E	E	E	E	E	E	E

41	42	43	44	45	46	47	48	49	50
A	A	A	A	A	A	A	A	A	A
B	B	B	B	B	B	B	B	B	B
C	C	C	C	C	C	C	C	C	C
D	D	D	D	D	D	D	D	D	D
E	E	E	E	E	E	E	E	E	E

51	52	53	54	55	56	57	58	59	60
A	A	A	A	A	A	A	A	A	A
B	B	B	B	B	B	B	B	B	B
C	C	C	C	C	C	C	C	C	C
D	D	D	D	D	D	D	D	D	D
E	E	E	E	E	E	E	E	E	E

61	62	63	64	65	66	67	68	69	70
A	A	A	A	A	A	A	A	A	A
B	B	B	B	B	B	B	B	B	B
C	C	C	C	C	C	C	C	C	C
D	D	D	D	D	D	D	D	D	D
E	E	E	E	E	E	E	E	E	E

71	72	73	74	75	76	77	78	79	80
A	A	A	A	A	A	A	A	A	A
B	B	B	B	B	B	B	B	B	B
C	C	C	C	C	C	C	C	C	C
D	D	D	D	D	D	D	D	D	D
E	E	E	E	E	E	E	E	E	E